I0020021

Visualization

Enhancing Imagination: A Comprehensive Manual On
Harnessing The Potential Of Visualization To Materialize
Your Boldest Aspirations

*(The Ultimate Creativity And Visualization Guide For
Learning More)*

Rodney Carpenter

TABLE OF CONTENT

An Overview Of Data Mining

I am confident that you may have been exposed to a multitude of discussions regarding the significance of data mining. Could you kindly provide a definition of data mining? Data mining, as its moniker implies, entails the identification and extraction of concealed patterns, variables, and trends from any collected dataset utilized for analysis purposes. In layman's terms, data mining, or knowledge discovery of data (KDD), refers to the process of analyzing data to detect and extract underlying patterns and trends that are valuable for categorizing and conducting meaningful analyses on the data. Data mining can be utilized to transform unprocessed data or information into a structured format that organizations can leverage for their operations.

It should be noted that organizations frequently gather and organize data from repositories known as data warehouses. They employ various data mining algorithms and efficacious analysis algorithms to arrive at well-informed determinations concerning their enterprise. By means of data mining, organizations have the capability to examine extensive amounts of data to discern patterns and trends that would be unattainable through rudimentary analysis algorithms. Our evaluation of data segments and calculation of the likelihood of future events are conducted through the utilization of sophisticated statistical and mathematical algorithms. Organizations employ data mining techniques to retrieve the requisite information from extensive databases or datasets in order to address various business inquiries or challenges.

Data mining and science exhibit similarities, and under certain circumstances, these processes can be executed by a single individual. These processes are always conducted with a specific objective in mind. Data science and data mining encompass a range of processes including web mining, text mining, video and audio mining, social media mining, and pictorial data mining. This task can be accomplished effortlessly using various software programs.

It is recommended for companies to engage in the practice of outsourcing data mining processes as it offers the advantage of reduced operational costs. Certain companies also utilize technology to acquire different types of data that cannot be retrieved through manual means. There is an abundance of data available across various platforms, yet the accessibility of meaningful insights derived from this data remains limited.

Every organization encounters challenges in conducting in-depth analyses of the diverse range of information gathered, in order to derive the essential insights required for problem-solving or informed business decision-making. A wide array of methodologies and tools can be employed to extract valuable insights from diverse sources of information.

Data Types Utilized in Data Mining

You can perform data mining on the following data types:

Relational Databases

Each database is structured using records, tables, and columns. A relational database pertains to a type of database system wherein you have the capability to gather information from diverse tables or data sets and structurally arrange it in the format of columns, records, and tables. One can readily retrieve this data without any concerns regarding specific data sets. The data is communicated and exchanged via tables that enhance the efficiency of arrangement, documentation, and retrieval.

Data Warehouses

Each enterprise gathers data from various sources in order to acquire information that aids in making sound and informed decisions. They can effortlessly accomplish this through the utilization of data warehousing methods. This substantial amount of data originates from various sources, including the fields of finance and marketing. The acquired data is subsequently utilized for the purpose of examination, which aids enterprises in making informed organizational choices. The primary purpose of the implemented data warehouse is to facilitate the analysis of data, as opposed to carrying out transactional processing.

Data Repositories

A data repository denotes the designated site where an organization can archive and preserve data. The majority of information technology professionals utilize this terminology to denote the configuration and acquisition of data within the organization. For instance, they refer to a cluster of databases that house diverse types of data.

Object-Relational Database

An object-relational database represents a fusion of a relational database and a model based on object-oriented principles. This database employs inheritance, classes, objects, and other similar constructs. The objective of this database is to bridge the divide between an object-oriented and relational database model through the utilization of various programming languages, such as C#, C , and Java.

Transactional Databases

A database management system, commonly referred to as a transactional database, possesses the capability to revert any transaction executed within the database, provided that it was not conducted in accordance with the proper protocols. This constitutes a distinctive ability that was established in prior times through the implementation of a relational database. These databases are the exclusive ones that facilitate such activities.

Advantages and Disadvantages of Data Mining

Pros

Data mining techniques facilitate the acquisition of insights and patterns from the dataset, empowering organizations to derive valuable information. They have the ability to utilize this information in order to make well-informed decisions that benefit the organization.

By means of data analysis, enterprises are able to implement the requisite alterations in their production and operational processes.

Data mining is comparatively less costly in comparison to alternative methods of statistical data analysis.

Enterprises have the capacity to unveil obscured trends and patterns within the dataset while also being able to compute the likelihoods associated with the manifestation of particular trends.

Due to the streamlined and efficient nature of data mining, the integration of this methodology into a new or established platform can be accomplished in a timely manner. The utilization of data mining methodologies and algorithms enables the examination of substantial quantities of data within a concise timeframe.

Cons

Data privacy and security are paramount considerations in the realm of data mining. Enterprises have the ability to monetize the data of their clientele by transferring it to other firms in exchange for financial gain. American Express has monetized the transactions made by their customers by selling them to external entities.

The majority of data mining software employs complex and sophisticated algorithms for operation, necessitating users to undergo the necessary training to effectively work with these models.

Varied models operate according to diverse algorithms and concepts, resulting in distinct functionalities. Hence, it is of utmost importance to select the appropriate data mining model.

Certain data mining techniques may not yield accurate outcomes, which can give rise to significant consequences.

Utilizations of Data Mining

The application of data mining is prevalent among organizations that face high levels of consumer expectations. Among the various sectors encompassed are communication, retail, marketing, finance, and so forth. "They utilize it for the subsequent purposes:

To ascertain customer preferences

Comprehend the means by which customers can attain satisfaction.

Evaluate the influence of different procedures on sales performance.

The strategic placement of commodities within the company

Evaluate strategies to enhance profitability

Retail establishments have the opportunity to utilize data mining techniques to formulate targeted promotions and create innovative products, thereby garnering attention and drawing in their customer base. This section encompasses several realms in which data mining is extensively employed.

Healthcare

Utilizing analytics and data to glean enhanced insights from datasets, data mining possesses the capacity to enhance various facets of the healthcare system. The healthcare sector can utilize this data to discern the appropriate services for enhancing healthcare provision while also diminishing expenses. Additionally, many enterprises employ data mining methodologies, including techniques such as data visualization, machine learning, soft computing, statistical analysis, and multi-dimensional databases, to analyze a variety of datasets and predict the classification of patients across various categories. These data mining procedures facilitate the healthcare sector in effectively delivering timely and location-specific intensive care to patients. Data extraction and analysis additionally empowers insurers to detect instances of misconduct and fraudulent activities.

Analysis of Consumer Trends and Shopping Patterns

This mode of analysis is grounded on various conjectures. If you opt to acquire particular items, there is a high likelihood that you will also acquire another item within the same product category. This methodology of analysis facilitates the identification of the purchasing patterns exhibited by individual customers within the customer cohort, thereby assisting retailers in discerning customer purchasing behavior. The retailer can also utilize this data to discern the preferences and requirements of buyers or customers, thereby facilitating modifications to the store's arrangement. One could also engage in a comparative analysis of various establishments, facilitating a more distinct categorization of diverse consumer segments.

Education

The application of data mining in the field of education is relatively nascent, with the primary aim being the extraction and examination of insights from vast quantities of data in educational settings. The utilization of educational data mining (EDM) enables the examination of the influence of different educational systems and support on a student, thereby facilitating an understanding of the student's future behavior. Educational institutions employ data mining techniques to inform informed decision-making processes aimed at facilitating student progress. Additionally, data mining techniques are employed to forecast a student's academic outcomes. Educational institutions can utilize this information to discern the appropriate curriculum for a student. Additionally, this information can be utilized to establish effective instructional approaches for educating students.

Manufacturing Engineering

Each manufacturing enterprise is required to possess an understanding of customer preferences, and this knowledge serves as a valuable asset for them. One can leverage a range of data mining tools to effectively discern concealed patterns and trends across diverse manufacturing processes. One could additionally employ data mining techniques to facilitate the development of suitable company designs and identify potential correlations between product portfolios and architecture. You have the opportunity to integrate diverse customer specifications in order to cultivate a framework that serves the interests of both the enterprise and the clientele. This data can subsequently be utilized to project product development, expenses, and delivery schedules, among other parameters.

Ensure A Comprehensive Understanding Of Your Personal Vision

After determining a specific daily schedule for meditation and affirming your dedication to it, the subsequent phase entails establishing a definitive understanding of your individual vision. It is crucial for you to have a comprehensive understanding of this chapter as it contains the key information. This is your objective. If you lack clarity in this matter, then all the time spent on meditation will be futile.

Although the pursuit of profound serenity and tranquility is undoubtedly commendable, the primary aim of this book is to augment your concentration abilities to such an extent that you can manifest your own unique subjective perception of reality through the practice of creative visualization. In order for this to occur, it is imperative that you possess a lucid understanding of the alternative reality that you envision for your own circumstances.

What precise vision do you possess? Please bear in mind the following concerns, as it is quite effortless to yearn for 'change' and inadvertently find oneself in a more unfavorable state. Why? Lack of proper definition.

Everyone possesses aspirations and desires.

The initial aspect that I wish for you to comprehend is that the possession of hopes and desires does not inherently grant you a personal vision. Mere aspirations and desires do not suffice. Hopes and wishes typically encompass indefinite sentiments for favorable transformation in the forthcoming period or a longing for beneficial occurrences to manifest in one's life.

Although I can comprehend and appreciate the emotional intensity associated with harboring hopes and wishes, it is crucial to be mindful that one's focus should not solely be fixated on the transient relief experienced during such aspirations for a more favorable existence. Given the circumstances, it is apparent that the majority of individuals possess aspirations and desires; however, they often find themselves incapable of effecting substantial transformations in their lives. Why? Hopes and aspirations alone are insufficient.

When individuals entertain hopes and aspirations, they are essentially engaging in fanciful musings. They are essentially seeking respite from the vexations of their everyday lives. They are cognizant of their unhappiness. They are cognizant of the need for a transformative shift in their lives, hence they harbor aspirations and desires for fortuitous advancements. They hold an earnest aspiration and desire for an amelioration of their life circumstances, often within an impractical timeframe, leading to a mere cathartic solace amidst profound dismay or even despondency caused by their present predicament.

However, once individuals experience the sensation of relief, they cease their actions. Expressing optimism and yearning alone fails to incentivize individuals to proactively engage or transform their perspectives that prompt tangible behavioral modifications. The rationale behind their behavior is their pursuit of a means to seek emotional solace. Therefore, it is of utmost significance to prioritize the cultivation of a distinct personal vision for oneself. A personal vision can be likened to possessing an emotive and psychological navigational guide.

In the absence of a cartographic tool and navigational instrument, one finds oneself in a state of disorientation.

Even in the absence of a map and compass, if one appears to be "traveling" aimlessly, they are indeed experiencing a state of being lost. You appear to be engaged in a pattern of circular activity without a clear sense of the progress being achieved. One cannot ascertain if they are approaching their destination or moving away from it. You have no clue. You are merely carrying out actions without genuine engagement.

Take note that you are exerting considerable effort. You are engaging in proactive measures, hence you are progressing step by step. However, in the absence of a map and compass, such endeavors become futile, as they lack direction and purpose, rendering them ultimately fruitless. The cultivation of a personal vision equips individuals with both a guide and a navigational tool to manifest the desired alternate reality into their actual lived experiences.

To put it in more sophisticated terms, when you condense your personal vision, you elucidate it to such an extent that it functions as both a navigational tool and a guiding principle. It is exceedingly difficult to experience confusion when one possesses a distinctly lucid and precisely articulated personal vision. What is the process/tactic/methodology to accomplish this task? How can one construct a personal vision that serves as a guiding force, enabling them to gauge their actions in a manner that brings them nearer to their ultimate aspirations, instead of engaging in aimless endeavors? Here's how.

Assume the role of a journalist

The initial step in establishing your personal vision is to perceive it as a form of enigma. Journalists and investigators possess superior skills in unraveling enigmatic conundrums. Their intellectual superiority is not the reason for their success; instead, it is attributed to the effectiveness of their systematic approach. If one is inclined to ascertain their personal vision with clarity, they could adopt a journalist's approach by employing the inquisitive aspect of the five W's and one H, as commonly employed by reporters.

The five aforementioned W's encompass the inquiry of identifying the individuals involved, the nature of the subject matter, the specified time frame, the designated location, and the underlying reasons for a given phenomenon. The letter H represents the concept of 'how'. Now, I kindly request that you reflect upon your aspirations, expectations, and any additional musings regarding an alternative existence that you desire for yourself. Just know yourself out. Please enumerate the alternate lifestyles that you wish to experience. To what extent would it deviate from your existing lifestyle? Direct your attention solely towards these alternate options.

Upon completion of recording your initial thoughts, the subsequent action entails documenting the individuals associated with your envisioned life, followed by delineating the nature and essence of that ideal existence. Similarly, with regards to location, could you please specify the geographical coordinates of the alternate reality you aspire to materialize in your life? At what juncture would you prefer to witness the realization of these events? Is it realistic? Do the objectives in question pertain to minor milestones or secondary time constraints?

Ultimately, it becomes imperative to inquire as to the rationale behind this vision. Why not something else? This may present a challenge as it will require you to engage in utmost self-honesty. Are you interested in an alternate state of existence that conforms to the desires of others? Do you frequently view video footage featuring individuals aboard luxury yachts or private jets, and have you expressed a desire to emulate such a lifestyle? Alternatively, are you simply conforming to or assimilating the wishes of others? It must belong to you. It is imperative that it possesses logical coherence to your understanding.

You must contemplate the reasons and scrutinize your motivations in order to gain complete clarity on the alternative reality that you should genuinely pursue.

Ultimately, it is imperative to inquire about the method or approach one should utilize in order to accomplish this task. In a highly practical manner, inquire within yourself, "what measures can I take to transform this individualistic aspiration into actuality?" For instance, when considering your individual vision of residing in an opulent $6 million mansion within the Hollywood hills, it becomes evident that procuring the necessary funds is the initial course of action. I am not solely referring to the financial aspect of purchasing the house, but rather, I am also encompassing the need to secure funds for covering property tax, maintenance expenses, and other expenditures linked to the overall cost of owning the property in question.

It is imperative that you consider these parameters. Do not solely fixate on the attractive vehicle, the splendid holiday, the expansive abode, or the impressive physique that you diligently build within the confines of the gymnasium for your personal satisfaction. Additionally, give attention to devising a plan for achieving your goals. Upon careful contemplation, one could discern that the question of "how" pertains to the process of mapping out the route from point B, denoting the ultimate destination of one's vision, to point A, representing the current position. One must simply retrace their steps starting from the final destination. It is essential to consistently inquire yourself about the frequency of how often one should repetitively examine the question in order to avoid any omissions in the process.

One must refrain from making any leaps of faith. In order to ensure the utmost realism, it is imperative to carefully navigate the path from the ultimate objective or ultimate vision, all the way to the present circumstance. In broad terms, if your aspiration entails leading a comfortable lifestyle replete with various material acquisitions, it becomes imperative to devise a strategy for generating the necessary financial resources. Subsequently, you should undertake a systematic analysis to comprehensively discern and outline the requisite steps to be taken.

For instance, revisiting the mansion scenario, it will be necessary to secure a sum of $6 million in addition to potentially allocating $2 million for miscellaneous expenses, resulting in a total of $8 million. What is your approach to acquiring those funds? Subsequently, you may contemplate your present actions. Maybe you design websites. Instead of engaging in client-based design work, it may be prudent to consider creating lucrative websites for personal gain. Thus, an initial amount of $8 million serves as the basis for further analysis, wherein the task at hand is to determine the number of income generating websites needed to yield $8 million, as well as the corresponding time required to achieve this goal, and so forth.

Within this context, you are employing the term "how" to systematically deconstruct the various stages that distinguish your present existence from the envisioned life you aspire to manifest. This is the method by which one ensures the maintenance of realism. One cannot engage in blind leaps of faith, hoping that one day they will fortuitously possess the winning lottery ticket they happened to purchase. That plan is not well-founded. I trust that it is evident to you.

Ensuring the absence of any logical gaps is imperative. You must refrain from entertaining unrealistic hopes or assuming that immense financial opportunities will effortlessly materialize, such as the sudden acquisition of a multi-million dollar account. That is not the functioning principle. That's not realistic. I am not affirming the absence of this occurrence. I am confident that there may be occasional occurrences of this nature, however, it is impractical to base one's life plans on the probability of a highly improbable event taking place. Do you comprehend the essence of this matter?

Once more, analyze and evaluate your underlying intentions

Presently, it is likely that you have developed a rather intricate conception of yourself. Before we proceed any further, it would be beneficial for you to undertake an additional evaluation of your underlying motivations to ascertain their authenticity in aligning with personal aspirations. It is imperative that you ascertain your sincere desire for pursuing your personal vision. Not due to your mere attempts to imitate or replicate the lives of others. It is imperative to establish unequivocally that your motivation stems from aspects that possess genuine pertinence and specificity to your own circumstances.

Comprehend the ramifications of your desires.

Once you have identified your personal vision, with a well-defined trajectory from your current situation to the desired outcome, the subsequent task is to comprehend the consequences associated with the vision. It is one matter to aspire to possess a luxurious Mercedes Benz or a prestigious Ferrari. It is a different matter altogether to acquire a full understanding of the sacrifices and diligent efforts required to procure such possessions.

Comprehend the ramifications of your vision, as the inquiry it elicits is, in essence, quite uncomplicated. Are you prepared to dedicate the necessary time, exertion, and relinquishments in order to materialize that vision? To what extent do you desire it? Do you comprehend the level of effort required to attain that alternative state of existence? It is imperative that you grasp this concept, as without implications, all that remains is a meticulously constructed illusion—nothing more. The presence of implications clarifies that certain obligations will be expected of you.

Repetitive encounters with adversity and obstacles will be necessary before ultimately prevailing. It necessitates a display of patience on your part. It necessitates careful allocation of your time and resources. In order to obtain the necessary funds to establish a company that will facilitate the realization of your aspirations, it would be necessary for you to forego enjoyable pastimes such as socializing with friends and engaging in leisurely activities, and instead dedicate extensive periods of time to the pursuit of occupational endeavors. Are you able to perceive the mechanics of this process? Implications are crucial. It is imperative that you do not omit this step, as it serves to determine the corresponding cost you are obligated to bear.

Final reminder

I must provide you with this ultimate notification. As you may have discerned, from a logical standpoint, the preceding step is indeed the final one. However, prior to our conclusion, it is imperative that I impart this ultimate reminder to you. It is essential to thoroughly articulate and establish a comprehensive personal vision while ensuring absolute clarity in its particulars. It is imperative to possess a well-crafted map that delineates the trajectory from one's present state to the envisioned future. However, it is essential to fully grasp the ramifications of one's desires and be prepared to bear the associated costs.

Without implementing that step, one's contemplations would be rendered mere idle fantasies. You are merely relying on hope and desire. Indeed, although your aspirations and desires are well-defined and easily discernible, it is highly unlikely that they will come to fruition given your lack of emotional commitment towards the indispensable sacrifices and exhaustive efforts necessary to realize your ambitions.

There must exist a moment of dedication. It is imperative to establish a genuine connection with the emotions involved. By way of explanation, it is not sufficient to merely express a willingness to engage in various tasks or responsibilities. To put it differently, this type of response only reflects a cognitive understanding, lacking genuine commitment or readiness. That's not enough. It is imperative that there be an emotional component involved. It is essential that you deeply internalize the commitment to embark on this journey. It will be characterized by a series of unexpected and intricate developments. The value will fluctuate. The journey ahead is bound to be challenging, necessitating personal sacrifices and endurance, yet, do you know what? The value of my aspiration is considerable. I am prepared to bear the cost.

That is the specific emotional condition which you must endeavor to attain. Otherwise, you're not visualizing. Alternatively, one would merely be relying on idle hopes and fleeting aspirations. There exists a distinction between engaging in daydreaming as a means of emotional refuge and engaging in genuine creative visualization. Let this distinction serve as your guide. The dissimilarity, in this case, lies in comprehending the ramifications and being prepared to bear the cost not solely in the realm of intellect but also experiencing it on an emotional plane.

Meditation And Visualization

In order to integrate the two forces of meditation and visualization, it is imperative to have cultivated experience in both beforehand. For individuals inexperienced in meditation, it is important to note that meditation provides numerous advantages, including the rejuvenation of energy levels and the cultivation of a state of focused tranquility. Hence, it should be evident to you that a correlation exists between meditation and visualization, as both facilitate concentration – one on achieving inner serenity and the other on identifying the elements necessary to cultivate personal contentment.

Meditation

Assume a posture of comfort. It is unnecessary to engage in intricate leg crossing during this particular form of meditation. You must be comfortable. Observing the placement of this lady's head, one can observe that it is ideally positioned to facilitate the inhalation of fresh air. If this entails being situated on your preferred shoreline or adjacent to your personal aquatic facility, then such a locale would be ideal; however, one may also pursue this activity within indoor premises. Please ensure that your attire does not impose limitations and that you are completely at ease prior to commencing the breathing exercises.

You will engage in nasal inhalation, retaining the breath within the abdominal region, and subsequently exhaling from the diaphragm for a marginally extended duration compared to the exhalation phase.

Consider it from this perspective:" or "Contemplate it in the following manner:

Inhale deeply, attentively perceiving the ingress of air into your being, and fully fixating your focus upon it – Enumerate to 8.

Maintain the air - Enumeration 6

Exhale utilizing the diaphragm - Engage in a counting sequence of up to 10.

Repeatedly perform the action, inhaling through the nostrils and exhaling through the mouth, while maintaining full mindfulness of the flow of air within your body. Divert your attention from any sources of disturbance. Your sole focus throughout this procedure ought to be centered exclusively on your respiration.

Once you have attained the capacity to exclusively focus on your breath, engage in this activity for a duration of approximately 10 minutes. This enhances cognitive acuity and facilitates optimal concentration. The oxygen circulating within your body will contribute to a soothing effect.

Visualization

Maintain a consistent posture, albeit this time, as you inhale, mentally contemplate the object or scenario you wish to depict. This has the potential to evoke a tranquil sentiment. It may encompass the sensation of achieving financial satisfaction or accomplishment, or it may pertain to any genuine yearning of your heart.

While inhaling, articulate phrases that strengthen the imagery you are envisioning. For instance:

"I feel great energy."

"I feel great wealth."

As you engage in expiration, you perceive the release of all that vitality emanating from your physical being into the external environment, ready to be replenished with each subsequent inhalation.

Ensuring the consistent integration of this visualization technique in your daily routine is crucial, as failure to do so may impede the realization of your intended objectives. Although it may have required me fifty years to develop proficiency in playing the piano at a concert standard, I achieved this by consistently reinforcing the concept. One possible rephrasing in a formal tone could be: "I could have prioritized the ongoing worldly matters in my life and forsaken the pursuit of my dream." If I had taken that course of action, it is possible that I would have never acquired the skill of piano playing. Nevertheless, the intensity of my dream or visualization was such that it assimilated into my very identity, and so should your desires.

In order for your visualizations to manifest and become reality, it is imperative that you integrate both meditation and visualization into your daily routine. Do not harbor aspirations for unattainable physical feats, for they shall remain beyond reach. To achieve curls on straight hair, it will be necessary to utilize curling methods. It does not pertain to one's physical appearance. It pertains to one's emotional state and the accomplishments attained throughout one's lifetime. If your desire is to enhance your personal beauty, it is indeed beneficial to engage in envisioning yourself as a paragon of beauty, as doing so will allow you to cultivate the harmonious essence that typically accompanies physical attractiveness.

Carefully observe an individual who catches your attention due to their exceptional beauty. Upon initial observation, one's perception is that the individual possesses remarkable beauty. What that individual likely possesses is remarkable charisma, which constitutes a distinct phenomenon. The slight asymmetry of her nose or the relatively smaller size of her eyes are inconsequential. She exudes an aura of beauty as it emanates from her inner being. Hence, it is within the realm of possibility for individuals to attain that sensation and effectively communicate it to others solely by cultivating a sincere belief in their own embodiment of their aspirations.

Visualization Techniques

Visualization techniques stimulate the cognitive faculties within our minds, harnessing its dormant capabilities to triumph and achieve objectives. Visualization is simply a cognitive process wherein we engage in the formation of mental images depicting our desired experiences. The power of our imagination reigns supreme, as it remains the singular element essential for the entirety of the process. Undoubtedly, imagination surpasses knowledge.

Knowledge has limits. Imagination is limitless. The power of imagination empowers us to envision and create the desired path of our existence, encompassing all concomitant experiences. It elates our emotions and instills a sense of gratification as we contemplate our aspirations. It is remarkable how unaware we were of the transformative potential hidden within our seemingly innocent imaginations, capable of resolving all our difficulties and propelling us to the pinnacle of success. Recognizing that imagination knows no bounds, to what extent do you believe you can push the boundaries of your capabilities?

Top-tier athletes employ visualization strategies to achieve high levels of success in their respective athletic disciplines. A scientific study conducted on four groups of athletes has yielded evidence indicating that individuals possessing exceptional visualization abilities are more inclined to achieve victory compared to those who rely solely on physical training. It is indisputable that the perceptions stored within our subconscious are congruent with the objective realities that transpire in the external realm.

Treasure Draw

The act of treasure drawing entails creating an image of an object or concept that holds a significant value or desirability to us. Typically, we proceed with illustrating it in cases where it is feasible to do so. We position it strategically in locations that afford us convenient daily visibility, such as on the kitchen wall, your bedroom ceiling, or the refrigerator door. Tactics for plotting your success offer an illuminating portrayal of your true aspirations, thereby enabling the manifestation of your objectives.

Reformed Memory Visualization

In order to address conflicts and mitigate lingering resentments, a method known as reformed memory visualization is employed. By utilizing this methodology, you are actively visualizing mental images wherein negative components are intentionally substituted with positive ones, particularly focusing on the emotion you imbue into these visualizations. Essentially, it transforms the adverse past in order to generate a favorable future. This offers significant support to individuals who have encountered unfortunate circumstances in their history. For example, instead of grieving over tragedies or assigning blame, there is a tendency to channel that emotion towards personal growth, perceiving it as a significant catalyst for one's life. After recalling the scene, endeavor to maintain composure and cultivate a sense of tranquility by engaging in deep and steady breaths. Recreating the identical scenes repeatedly will necessitate a significant amount of time, but ultimately, you will achieve success.

Open Visualization

The cognitive practice of mentally visualizing a film, where one assumes the role of the director, is referred to as the open visualization technique. Through this technique, individuals possess complete authority to manipulate and oversee the development of said mental movie. An environment imbued with solemnity and openness is highly conducive to an exercise in which a student can envisage the perspective of a distinctive pictorial encounter. Engaging in this endeavor is most enjoyable when accompanied by music.

Directed Visualization

Directed visualization can be defined as the technique wherein individuals select and immerse themselves in a mental representation, experiencing it with such intensity that it becomes indistinguishable from reality. Individuals employ the aforementioned visualization technique in order to identify an inner locus characterized by a profound alignment with their innate intuition. Individuals employing this particular form of visualization generate solutions by means of the scenes they have envisioned. Through the process of visualizing mental representations, individuals evoke inquiries as well as solutions within their cognitive faculties.

Examples

Visualization can serve as a valuable tool to guide an individual who is in a state of perplexity, assisting them in finding the appropriate path. You have the opportunity to engage in visualization seminars, during which a distinguished speaker imparts knowledge to assist you in maximizing your potential through the power of visualization, complementing the invaluable insights already gained from this book. Additionally, it should be noted that speakers have the capability to generate enthusiasm and charm through the use of eloquent and dynamic speech. Additionally, individualized sessions are offered for individuals seeking a more personalized approach to engage in visualization techniques. Moreover, engaging in a personalized session would effectively fulfill your specific requirements. Engaging in this introspective exploration can also have positive impacts on one's overall well-being. In due course, you will experience an improvement in your overall well-being, and you will observe a greater manifestation of beneficial transformations. Gaining knowledge through the utilization of visualization techniques will serve as a catalyst for rejuvenating one's cognitive and emotional well-being, subsequently facilitating the attainment of desired outcomes by means of personal development. By appropriately exercising self-discipline and honing one's intuition, individuals can pave the way towards obtaining the rewards that are rightfully theirs.

In order to enhance the effectiveness of your visualization technique and increase the outcome of the treasure draw, there are alternative methods you can employ apart from clarifying your objectives and the associated milestones during the process. Please be aware that it is not strictly necessary for you to physically depict the things you desire. Additionally, it is possible to extract images from magazines, such as an elegant residence, a pristine automobile, or any visual representation that encapsulates your desired aspirations. In the event that magazines are unavailable, alternative pictorial resources can be accessed through the Internet and subsequently printed. The subsequent task entails affixing them onto a visualization board. This object is an uncomplicated assemblage of a cardboard box or illustration board, featuring a collage depicting all the desired elements. The final step involves affixing it to the wall in a visible location for daily reference.

It should be observed that visualization and imagination share a fundamentally similar approach. To conceptualize something is merely to envision it. The human intellect is incredibly remarkable, possessing the capacity to perceive and comprehend the information conveyed through visual imagery, in conjunction with its cognitive functioning. The subconscious mind exhibits distinct behavioral and emotional responses to each visual stimulus it encounters. Initially, one may encounter difficulty in visualizing vibrant images; however, through a combination of perseverance and dedication, one can enhance their ability to do so. It is not imperative to possess expertise in the art of visualization, but it is of utmost importance to have a proficient grasp of the skill.

Could You Please Elucidate The Functioning Principles Behind The Utilization Of Visualization Techniques?

The failure of this visualization largely stems from our analysis of why and how it functions. It is a relatively straightforward task to generate skepticism regarding the effectiveness of visualization, irrespective of the frequency or intensity with which we concentrate on anticipating the outcome. We simply hold onto the hope that it will come to fruition, regardless of the circumstances.

The concept of utilizing visual imagery to achieve a better quality of life has gradually become a widely accepted notion exclusive to our society.

And subsequently, rather than endeavoring to inform ourselves about the plausible causes behind its malfunction, we simply abandon all efforts and relinquish our pursuit, thereby perpetuating a state of existence where the realization of our immense abilities remains unattainable.

In contemporary society, numerous renowned athletes incorporate creative visualization as an integral component of their training regimen.

It is imperative that we do not overlook the fact that visualization is precisely what we desire or require, and it will inevitably manifest.

In our everyday lives, there are methods to enhance our ability to run 1-2 miles at a faster pace. Specifically, dedicating one hour out of the four days in a given week to visualize ourselves running the miles more swiftly would lead to further progress and success.

Although daydreaming can indeed be beneficial when discussing the manifestation of our goals or desires.

By adhering to a dependable timetable and dedicating regular intervals specifically designated for the purpose of practicing creative visualization, one can reasonably expect to achieve significantly superior outcomes.

The Vision Board Was Not Successful In Yielding The Desired Results.

If the affirmations depicted on the vision board have proven ineffectual, it is likely due to a lack of conviction in their viability. The success or failure of your written work is greatly influenced by your mindset, and it is possible that you are not employing sufficiently impactful language to effectively engage your mind. Observe their actions and contemplate whether their behavior truly aligns with your aspirations and goals in life. Now, position the board before you in a tranquil setting and allocate daily time to its pursuit, diligently reciting the mantras that you have inscribed. It is not possible to instantaneously transform a pessimistic mindset into a positive one, and it is necessary to continually reinforce these affirmations until complete belief is achieved in every word inscribed on the boards. Allow me to provide you with a compelling illustration of the potential consequences that may arise when one takes such action.

Cynthia Stafford emerged as the recipient of a substantial $112 million prize through the utilization of the Law of Attraction in the realm of lottery winnings. She endured considerable hardships while raising her brother's children following his passing, and throughout the entirety of her YouTube video, she consistently emphasized that in order to achieve success, "one must envision themselves already in possession of whatever it is they desire in life." This is precisely the purpose of vision boards. When one holds steadfast beliefs, events transpire in accordance, with positive energy being instrumental in shaping one's life. Individuals possessing significant levels of vitality are drawn towards activities that exude noteworthy levels of energy. They also have a penchant for attracting individuals of elevated energy levels.

Cynthia meticulously recorded the precise tally of her triumph on a sheet of paper, and drew inspiration from the image of her children as she transitioned from a struggling mother to the accomplished individual she has become. She was able to discern the impact on the children, yet she did not perceive it as a venture with lasting implications. She observed that the children were experiencing immediate benefits. There are other individuals who also have narratives to share. It is highly recommended for you to peruse her narrative on YouTube while also exploring other narratives as they hold equal legitimacy. This statement holds substantial meaning, and once you relinquish faith in the contents inscribed on the vision board, the aspiration dissipates. Hence, it is imperative that you begin anew and wholeheartedly embrace this conviction. One can only attain the identity they desire by wholeheartedly embracing the beliefs articulated in their writing and vividly envisioning their life embodying the traits of that person.

Visualization encompasses the practice of shutting one's eyes and envisioning existence and its various aspects. Similar to how a child envisions themselves as an astronaut, you envision yourself embodying the person you aspire to be and emotionally connect with that experience. Without this deep inner pull towards your desired identity, you may not generate the necessary level of motivation and enthusiasm to accomplish it. The entire process of visualizing requires effort, yet this effort is indispensable in attaining the desired destination.

I have attained all that I have desired in my life as a consequence of my unwavering faith in the efficacy of visualization. Negative, I do not hold the distinction of being the wealthiest individual on the planet; nevertheless, it has never aligned with my personal aspirations. The ideals that guided my vision were imbued with a profound sense of inner bliss, tranquility, and accord, which, through a transformative shift in my mindset, I successfully materialized. A few years ago, I found myself in a state of persistent depression, which had plagued me for an extended period of time. Indeed, individuals experiencing depression tend to exhibit a pattern of recurrent hospital visits due to their persistent adherence to the self-perception and labeling as "depressed" or "a depressive individual." While it is important to acknowledge that not every case is identical, the underlying mentality within the human brain remains strikingly similar across individuals, thereby presenting the possibility for transformative change in one's identity. I ceased perceiving myself as a victim and instead assumed the role of the protagonist in my life's narrative. Consequently, I have reached a stage wherein all my aspirations align harmoniously, a testament to the affirmative energy I am capable of radiating. I possess a firm conviction in the Law of Attraction and shall endeavor to elucidate its principles.

If upon your entrance into a ballroom, one harbors unfavorable thoughts about their attire and hairstyle, it is likely that their overall energetic state or vibrational frequency will be diminished. You have low expectations. In the utmost scenario, there is a possibility that you might receive a request to partake in a dance alongside an individual whom others, regrettably, display minimal interest in engaging with. Why? It is not related to your outward appearance. It pertains to the emanations of vibrations that you emit. Adorn the identical dress and hairstyle on a young woman who exudes self-assurance, and she will not only elicit attention from suitors overlooked by others, but also attract partners of higher desirability. Therefore, it is not the attire or the hairstyle. It's the energy emitted.

Enter the ballroom exuding grace and poise, irrespective of others' opinions about your attire, for such matters hold little significance. Embrace an aura of jubilation, effortlessly attracting positive energy and delight. Gentlemen will take notice of your presence, and it is assuredly not due to your attire. The presence of undeniable assurance and joy emanating from within is what attracts the attention and allure of respectable individuals who yearn for the opportunity to engage in a dance with you. Energy is of utmost importance and employing visualization techniques can aid in attaining that energy. After acquiring it, it is crucial to retain it, which is where the utilization of a vision board becomes advantageous. It facilitates the retention of the attained vibrations.

The trajectory of your life is determined by the amplitude of your vibrations and the intensity of your energy. One's financial status may be meager, yet they can possess the vitality and exuberance reminiscent of prosperous and content individuals. One can attain wealth and possess an aura of empathy and approachability. To achieve your aspirations in life, you must align your vibrational frequency with that of the individual you strive to become.

Start Moving.

Having embraced the vision of achieving success, it is now opportune to actualize it. The accomplishment of success does not hinge solely on mere visualization, but rather necessitates taking action. Indeed, the act of visualizing effectively compels one to take action. It also enables mental liberation, facilitating the generation of solutions and ideas. Nevertheless, it remains within your purview to determine the means by which you will realize your plans and objectives. Here are some tips:

Relax. Please refrain from exerting undue pressure upon yourself to generate ideas. Compelling oneself hinders the capacity to engage in clear thinking. As you become increasingly at ease, a greater influx of ideas will manifest.

Please document your imaginative ideas. With consistent engagement in visualization techniques, one will begin to experience the manifestation of inventive concepts residing within their mind. Documenting them will aid in memory retention and prove beneficial in the future when addressing and resolving any challenges.

Think positive. Once you have accomplished your intended objectives, maintain a confident stance regarding the subsequent outcomes.

Let go. Please refrain from concerning yourself with the outcome arising from your chosen course of action or decision. In the event that outcomes fail to align with your intentions, refrain from feeling disheartened. Occasionally, an unsuccessful outcome has the potential to unveil a greater and more advantageous opportunity. You simply need to determine a resolution.

Update it. Should you successfully attain your prior objective, you may amend your vision statement accordingly, aiming for an even more ambitious and demanding goal. For instance, in the event that your objective is to accumulate $100,000 within a span of five years, and you successfully accomplish this objective, it would be appropriate to revise your vision statement to reflect a new target of $200,000. Revision is imperative for achieving long-term aspirations when one witnesses significant transformations in their life. In the event that your initial intention was to establish a prosperous career as a dancer within a decade, and subsequently you discover a heightened inclination towards pursuing a path as a vocalist, it is permissible to revise your long-term aspirations in consonance with your current passions.

Action Point:

Upon engaging in the process of visualization, it is imperative to record the inventive resolutions that have been generated in order to effectively attain one's objective.

What Items Might You Consider Including On Your Checklist?

Include Context

What are the essential components that should be included in a design checklist prior to commencing the data visualization process? The primary aspect that necessitates clarification is the fact that data visualization revolves around the concept of context. The provision of context is essential in effectively establishing the framework for your viewers or audience to comprehend your perspective and the conveyed message. It is imperative that you consistently furnish the context, rather than presuming that the audience possesses a preexisting comprehension. By adopting this approach, you ensure that your intended design and message are effectively received and internalized by your audience, rather than being merely dismissed or disregarded. It is essential to bear in mind that when encountering an isolated numerical figure or value, our cognitive faculties struggle to comprehend its meaning, leading to viewer perplexity.

Due to the inherent challenge the brain faces in comprehending isolated words or letters, it lacks the ability to effectively classify them. Determining the magnitude, quality, trend, or direction of a data point necessitates contextualization and comparison with other relevant figures. As a result, should you neglect to furnish context to your audience, it is highly probable that they will surmise one, thereby giving rise to innumerable potential interpretations. Insufficient contextual information will result in the intended message being obscured amidst confusion.

However, what qualifies as adequate context? The responsibility lies with you to determine which information is essential to present, and which can be omitted from the visualization. It is imperative to develop a capacity for impartiality and equilibrium. Achieving equilibrium between conveying one's message, accurately representing vital data, and mitigating any potential bias in the design or visualization of data entails the process of achieving bias equilibrium.

Know Your Audience

By possessing knowledge of your audience, guarantee that your data visualization effectively communicates with and establishes a connection with your intended viewers. Commencing your design process with this understanding will enable you to determine the course of action. A chart tailored to accommodate the specific needs and skills of corporate professionals would not be suitable for high school students, who possess varying levels of competency in data interpretation and analysis, among other factors. Hence, prioritizing your audience should be among your foremost considerations.

The extent to which you can precisely articulate and elaborate on your target audience will greatly enhance your ability to tailor your designs specifically for them and effectively facilitate communication. Attempting to communicate with a wide-ranging demographic will adversely impact the efficacy of your communication. You are more inclined to establish stronger connections by focusing your audience and directing your visual content towards a specific viewer. The sensation of a lack of connection between oneself and the intended audience can result in a design of remarkable quality being rendered unsuccessful. In addition, identifying a target audience will enhance the sensitivity, attractiveness, and informational value of your design. By prioritizing their needs and interests, you will acquire insights into how various audience segments typically interpret information.

Consider how familiar your audience is with data visualizations and how you explain your data. The more acquainted you are with your audience, the greater your capacity to create a visual representation that deeply connects with them. In the event that you find yourself addressing an audience unfamiliar with statistical terminology and technical jargon, it may be necessary to omit such language and instead elucidate your content using non-specialized language. Additionally, consider the amount of time that your audience has available to engage with your visual representation. If the audience possesses limited time, patience, and interest, opting for straightforward charts and visuals is advisable. However, in the event that your target audience possesses ample time and a strong inclination towards the subject matter, it is possible to employ interactive charts and intricately designed visuals without encountering any issues.

When you engage in design while considering a particular audience, you concentrate on discerning their preferences, aversions, and perspectives. Subsequently, one must ascertain the duration of time available for the audience to peruse the visualization, establish their specific information needs, evaluate their existing knowledge, and determine the particular information they anticipate the presenter to furnish. This is essential for the development of something that elicits a deep connection and favorable reaction among individuals.

Your subsequent deliberation should involve the anticipated emotional, educational, or behavioral response that you intend to elicit in your viewers through your visual presentation. Every data visualization serves a purpose. In the absence of any narrative, ethical lesson, or substantive content to impart to one's audience, it would be more advisable to refrain from creating any designs whatsoever. Every piece of information included in your visual presentation should be deserving of its position and effectively capture the attention of the audience.

Train Your Imagination!

The contents of this chapter are designed to facilitate the recalibration of your thought processes and the revitalization of your imaginative capabilities. Through the practice of meditation and the cultivation of a mindset that perceives things from new perspectives, one can effectively develop the ability to envision and ultimately attain their desired outcomes and the sought-after success in life. Employing these resources will enable you to establish a suitable foundation for the implementation of creative visualization, ensuring that it becomes a gratifying, enjoyable, and prosperous pursuit for you.

In addition to honing your newfound meditation abilities, it would be advantageous to focus your efforts on enhancing your imaginative faculties. During one's childhood, there is an inherent ability to envision and create without limitations. However, the process of maturing often extinguishes this aptitude within many individuals. The utilization of creative visualization necessitates the inclusion of imagination as a fundamental component in the attainment of success.

Change Your Perspective

It is highly advisable for one to initiate a paradigm shift in their perception of reality, pushing the boundaries of their imagination to its utmost capabilities. Allocate a portion of your daily schedule to engage in unconventional thinking. Consider the potential reality if you were to assume the form of an animal. Do not dwell superficially; instead, diligently direct your focus towards the intricacies of the matter at hand. Imagine yourself in scenarios that are impossible to achieve, such as being located at the profoundest depths of the ocean or navigating through outer space devoid of a protective suit. When endeavoring to view matters from alternative vantage points, it is imperative to ensure that one is actively constructing one's reality. This is somewhat akin to the in-depth exploration of creative visualization that we will delve into later, although it primarily serves as a pleasurable pursuit for augmenting your imagination.

Derive pleasure from the uncomplicated elements.

The augmentation of a child's playfulness and enjoyment doesn't necessitate the introduction of intricate mechanisms or concepts. Consider devoting a day to solitude and endeavor to observe the world with the innocence and curiosity of a young individual. Engage in outdoor activities and disregard any concerns regarding perceptions from others. Consider the progression in which a child transitions from creating an artistic representation to engaging in imaginative play as an animal and subsequently transforming seemingly useless material into a purposeful creation. They engage in the discovery of uncomplicated objects or activities and transform them according to their own desires. It is within your capabilities to accomplish this as well. Although you might initially experience a sense of foolishness and displacement, it is precisely the desired outcome, and therefore, I encourage you to delight in it.

Commence to diligently observe all matters.

Please allot a brief pause to carefully observe the surroundings. Irrespective of one's activities throughout the day, one ought to contemplate the visual and tactile aspects, as well as other pertinent factors, associated with their surroundings. Observe your environment and conduct a thorough examination of the objects present. Direct your focus towards the authentic sensations of the wind, the genuine hues of your surroundings, and the diverse textures that evoke touch. This exercise holds significance due to its ability to enhance the efficacy of visualizations, as one can achieve greater success by delving into intricate details and genuinely experiencing the desired outcomes.

Please indulge in leisure activities or engage in playful pastimes.

Commence the integration of novel recreational activities into your daily routine. Discover enjoyable puzzle games or indulge in those that demand critical thinking and employ imaginative reasoning to successfully complete the given challenges. These tools can facilitate the exploration of new perspectives, enabling the expansion of one's imaginative capacities beyond conventional paradigms.

Start journaling

For individuals seeking to broaden their perspectives and transform their experiences, it is advised to commence a personal journal. This practice will enable the diligent recording of inventive ideas and musings. It can also be employed for sketching or objects that ignite a sense of inspiration. It will assist in redirecting your energy towards more innovative pursuits.

Taking meticulous care with respect to details.

Commence by acquiring a sheet of paper, a pencil, and a magazine. Select a page arbitrarily and direct your attention to the visual depiction. Upon the elapse of 1 minute, proceed to promptly shut the periodical and initiate the act of transcription. Create a comprehensive inventory of all elements within the picture by recalling them from memory. Subsequently, conduct a thorough review of the list to ascertain its completeness and accuracy, ensuring that no additional details were omitted or errors were made. It is feasible to engage in this exercise multiple times throughout the day, requiring only a small amount of spare time. With consistent practice, you will quickly observe an increase in the number of items you include in your list each time.

Start New Hobbies

Consider incorporating novel activities into your daily routine. Embark on day excursions to unfamiliar destinations in your vicinity, explore novel pastimes, or engage in literary works outside your customary repertoire. It is imperative to observe novel occurrences and engage in unfamiliar experiences in order to transcend the confines of routine. Commencing this task should pose no significant difficulty, albeit, it is crucial to continuously bear in mind that your objective is to create space for novel experiences and venture beyond your accustomed and cozy domain.

Activities For Cultivating Your Imagination

In addition to acquiring proficiency in meditation, it would be essential for you to focus on fostering the development of your imagination. During childhood, individuals possess the remarkable ability to conceive unlimited possibilities and construct imaginative concepts in their minds. However, as individuals mature, this inherent capability often becomes diminished or extinguished. The utilization of imaginative faculties through the practice of creative visualization plays a crucial role in attaining success. Presently is the opportune moment for you to reclaim that imagination which has been misplaced and acquire the skill to effectively utilize its potential. Therefore, let us explore a selection of exercises that can facilitate its restoration and growth for you.

Engage in novel pursuits.

Consider incorporating novel activities into your daily routine. Embark on day excursions to unexplored locales in close proximity, cultivate novel interests or literature genres that deviate from your customary preferences. It is crucial to observe novel aspects and engage in new experiences in order to facilitate a departure from ingrained routines. Commencing with this task should pose moderate difficulty, however, it is necessary to continuously bear in mind that your objective is to create space for novel experiences in your life and venture beyond your customary and comfortable boundaries.

Take pleasure in the modest aspects of life.

Children do not require intricate objects or activities in order to enhance the playfulness or enjoyment of their lives. Consider allocating a day for personal reflection and observing the world through the lens of youthful innocence and curiosity. Engage in recreational activities without concern for the perception of others. Consider the developmental process that enables a child to progress from illustrating a picture to engaging in imaginative play as a monkey to transforming seemingly discarded objects into meaningful creations. They discover elementary pleasures and adeptly mold them into desired forms. It is within your capability to accomplish this as well. Although you may initially experience a sense of foolishness and a feeling of not belonging, this is precisely the intended outcome, therefore, embrace it with delight.

Play some games.

Commence the integration of novel games into your daily routine. Explore enjoyable puzzle games, specifically those that challenge your logical thinking and stimulate imaginative problem-solving skills necessary to successfully complete the assigned tasks. These methodologies have the potential to enhance your imaginative capabilities by facilitating novel modes of thought beyond your accustomed approaches.

Start keeping a journal.

In your pursuit of broadening your perspectives and transforming your perception of the world, it would be prudent to commence the practice of maintaining a personal journal. Jot down all your imaginative ideas. This tool can also be employed for sketching or capturing objects that evoke a sense of inspiration. It will assist in directing your efforts towards more imaginative endeavors.

Direct your attention to every detail.

Please pause and carefully observe your surroundings. Irrespective of your daily engagements, I urge you to contemplate the visual aesthetics, tactile sensations, and all other aspects pertaining to your surroundings. Observe the environment that surrounds you and carefully analyze the objects within it. Give careful consideration to the genuine sensation of the wind, the authentic hues in every element, and the entirety of the tactile qualities you experience. This exercise proves to be crucial due to the enhanced levels of success one can achieve by diligently and meticulously envisioning their goals, delving into intricate details, and genuinely immersing oneself in the desired experiences.

Commence engaging in some training methodologies.

There exist a plethora of exercises which are purposefully crafted to cultivate and rekindle the imaginative capacities that were once joyfully embraced during childhood. Although these tasks typically require only a brief portion of your busy schedule, their potential benefits make them highly worthwhile investments of your time. Here are several approaches that you can experiment with.

Paying Attention to Details

Begin by acquiring a sheet of paper, a writing instrument, and a publication. Randomly select a page and direct your attention to the accompanying image. Upon the completion of 60 seconds, proceed to shut the magazine and commence the act of writing. Please compile a comprehensive inventory of all elements discernible in the image.

Subsequently, conduct a revisionary examination to identify any potential omissions or inaccuracies. You may engage in the repetition of this exercise multiple times daily, allocating only a small portion of your free time. Before long, you will discern a notable increase in the number of items that you are able to add to your list with each subsequent iteration.

Change Your Perspective

It is imperative that you strive to alter your cognitive framework regarding your perceived reality and endeavor to extend the boundaries of your imagination to their utmost capacity. Allocate a portion of your daily schedule for the purpose of stretching your cognitive abilities and exploring unconventional perspectives. Consider the hypothetical scenario of adopting the perspective of an animal. Do not limit your thinking to superficial observations; rather, prioritize a thorough analysis of the intricacies of the given situation. Envision yourself in scenarios that lie beyond the realms of possibility, such as being submerged in the depths of the ocean or traversing the vast expanse of space without proper attire. When endeavoring to adopt alternative viewpoints, ensure that you are actively constructing the framework of the world in which you exist. This practice bears some resemblance to the concept of creative visualization that we will delve into more extensively. However, it primarily serves as a leisurely pursuit aimed at fostering and expanding one's imaginative capacity.

All the contents encompassed within this chapter have been curated with the intent of assisting you in the process of reshaping your cognitive perspectives and revitalizing the potency of your imaginative potential. Through the practice of meditation and the cultivation of a cognitive perspective shift, you will acquire the necessary tools to envision your desired outcomes with clarity and manifest the abundant success you aspire to in your personal and professional life. Utilizing these resources will establish an appropriate foundation for engaging in creative visualization, ensuring that it becomes a pleasurable, enjoyable, and fruitful pursuit for you.

Creative Visualization And Meditation

With the advent of the widely embraced documentary known as "The Secret," a multitude of individuals have endeavored to employ visualization techniques in order to manifest their aspirations and ambitions. Nevertheless, there are individuals who assert that despite dedicating hours every day to envisioning their goals and desires, their manifestations failed to materialize in the realm of tangible reality.

The act of visualizing possesses profound potential to bring forth desired outcomes and aspirations in one's life. Nevertheless, it is imperative to execute the task with precision in order to effectively harness its potential to transform your aspirations and desires into tangible outcomes.

Creative visualization constitutes a systematic procedure. It entails harnessing the potential of one's thoughts to attain desired aspirations. You do not simply engage in fantasy or indulge in idle reverie. When engaging in visualization, one purposefully directs their thoughts in order to actualize their aspirations and goals.

"The Creative Visualization Process comprises four essential components:
Meditation
Visualization
Affirmation
Acknowledgement and Gratitude
Inspired Action

Within this chapter, we shall delve into the initial aspect of the Creative

Visualization procedure, namely, the practice of meditation. We shall address the remaining components in the subsequent chapters.

Meditation

The initial stage of the creative visualization process involves engaging in meditation and achieving a state of mental tranquility. Prior to entertaining any thoughts or envisioning your desired outcome, it is imperative to achieve a state of mental tranquility and prepare your mind, ensuring it is suitably attuned for the entirety of the creative visualization process. Meditation additionally contributes to enhancing your ability to concentrate and maintain a higher degree of mental imagery retention. Meditation contributes to the enhancement of cognitive fortitude and the cultivation of mental dexterity. Meditation constitutes a cognitive exercise aimed at sharpening one's mental faculties, thereby facilitating the utilization of the latent potential of the subconscious mind to effectively materialize desired outcomes in life. Outlined are several methods that can be employed to facilitate meditation or prepare the mind for visualization.

Cultivate a optimistic outlook

Prior to embarking upon the deliberate act of envisioning one's wants and desires, it is imperative to ascertain the presence of a positive cognitive framework. It is imperative to eradicate uncertainties and doubt. It is imperative to maintain the belief that engaging in Creative Visualization will profoundly alter one's destiny in a positive manner.

One must hold the belief that they possess all the necessary qualities and capabilities to engage in purposeful endeavors aimed at realizing their aspirations and goals. A highly efficacious approach to achieve this would be to engage in deliberate visualization. What is your thought process when you consider the concept of visualization? Do you possess any pessimistic thoughts or emotional reactions regarding the matter? Do you have doubts? If doubts and negative perceptions regarding visualization exist, it is crucial to promptly attend to them. It is imperative that you alter your perception by substituting negative thoughts with positive ones. Consistently instill this affirmation within the depths of your subconscious – "The practice of creative visualization shall successfully manifest my aspirations into tangible outcomes."

Choose a specific time and location that would allow you to direct your attention effectively.

It is recommended that you engage in your daily meditation and visualization exercise during the mornings. This is due to the state of relaxation that your mind attains in the morning, when worries have yet to occupy your thoughts, and your mind remains unburdened by work and the stresses associated with relationships. In order to expedite outcomes, it is advisable to engage in this activity a minimum of two times per day. During the early hours after awakening and in the late hours preceding sleep. It is recommended to allocate a minimum of 5 minutes each day for engaging in meditation, supplemented by an additional 10 minutes devoted to envisioning and bringing to life the desired impressions of one's ideal future.

Additionally, it is imperative to designate a location where you can work without any interruptions. In an ideal scenario, it is advisable to perform this activity within the confines of your bedroom. Select a suitable location where you may engage in meditation and visualization. Make this corner special. Please position either a cushion or a notably comfortable chair within this corner. Additionally, you have the option to arrange flowers or display cherished objects, such as seashells, lamps, or figurines. Please ensure that the environment is both comfortable and tranquil. Please close the windows and ensure that the room is maintained at an optimal temperature. If desired, it is possible to position an altar or arrange floral decorations within this specific area.

Direct Your Focus towards Your Respiration

Once you have fully prepared and achieved a state of comfort, gently shut your eyes and inhale deeply a few times. Inhale. Exhale. It is advisable to engage in the practice of taking five deep abdominal breaths. Direct your focus solely on your respiration. Maintain a state of mental calm and refrain from any extraneous thoughts. Direct your attention solely to your breath. Breathe in and out. When you engage in this action, a greater volume of air will be able to ingress into your pulmonary system, leading to the subsequent relaxation of your diaphragm. Ensure that you are appropriately engaging in respiratory processes and, of greater significance, direct your exclusive attention to the act of breathing. Should your thoughts begin to stray, redirect your focus to your breath. This may initially pose a moderate level of difficulty, yet as familiarity is acquired, the outcomes achieved will astonish you. It is within your capacity to regulate your emotions and enhance your concentration. Notably, the subconscious mind has a heightened receptivity to assimilate the visual stimuli that will be imprinted through visualization.

Envision a luminous white beam

Maintain the position of closing your eyes and envision a brilliant luminescent glow emanating from the space directly above your head. Visualize yourself being encompassed by that radiant glow. May the radiance permeate your entire essence, imbuing it with tranquility, harmony, and affection. Allow it to permeate each individual cell within your physical body, every intricately woven tissue, and every vital organ. Continue to breathe. Please proceed with counting from one to twenty-five, and once you have achieved a state of relaxation, you may begin to engage in visualization.

Deliberating Upon The Selection Of Manifestations

Synopsis

The assertion, "One has the potential to achieve anything through sheer determination," implies that by visualizing one's desired goals, committing wholeheartedly to the endeavor, and patiently persevering, triumph is assured.

To a certain extent, this remains true. The convergence of a well-defined goal and proactive efforts yields a formidable influence. However, the statement is misleading as it fails to address the issue and the importance of directing one's attention towards a specific objective.

What are your desires and preferences?

The majority of individuals lack clarity regarding their desires. Our team maintains the stance that we do, notwithstanding, we sincerely do not. We merely acknowledge our preferences. We desire work of exceptional quality. We have no inclination to be destitute. We aim to ensure that our household is content and fulfilled.

Understanding precisely your desires is significantly more diverse than discerning your dislikes. When one possesses a comprehensive understanding of one's dislikes, it becomes evident that their objectives lack focus and they manifest unfavorably. Consider this image.

Expenses do not wish to be devoid of funds. He is troubled by the fact that he earns less than his close acquaintances, and he is determined to improve his circumstances. In order to achieve this goal, Bill has the opportunity to enroll in a diverse array of courses. He possesses the qualifications to offer instruction for lucrative occupations, such as that of a physician or lawyer. He has the potential to establish his own business, engage in real estate ventures, or pursue numerous other endeavors that can lead to wealth creation.

However, Bill remains uncertain regarding his intentions. He lacks an understanding of the optimal course that aligns with his abilities and personal traits, thereby refraining from committing to any specific path.

With the purpose of addressing this query, he explores various prospects. However, upon encountering difficulties, he determines that the path is not suitable for him and proceeds towards an alternative avenue.

Expense's activities aren't focused. Whilst his responsibilities are undoubtedly challenging, it can be observed that his endeavors fail to generate mutual enhancement.

Instead of building a singular, large, impenetrable sandcastle, Bill has actually raised and nurtured a group of 20 well-behaved children who are conveniently at his disposal. He finds himself perplexed and disheartened. In essence, Bill's lack of emphasis leads to failure.

Presently, what would be the outcome if Bill were to have selected a particular course of action and set specific objectives to manifest? He had the intention of pursuing a career in the field of regulation. His actions and indicators of presence would have been clearly outlined

· Achieve a higher score on the Law School Admission Test

· Obtain letters of recommendation

· Attain acceptance to a prestigious law school

· Select a specific branch of law

· Achieve a standard level of compliance

· Seek an employment opportunity in a prestigious legal firm with generous remuneration.

Attaining a set of specific objectives proves considerably less intricate and more attainable in contrast to the ambiguous goal of acquiring wealth. Having a strong focus on a particular path enables individuals to meticulously plan a set of logical and purposeful actions in order to achieve desired outcomes. Every achievement brings us one step closer to the ultimate goal.

I believe it is likely that we can all agree that committing to a clearly defined path towards success, regardless of its nature, offers Expense the greatest chance of achieving prosperity.

However, how can he possibly make a decision on a course of action if he lacks clarity regarding his desires? Perhaps financial gain is not his sole motivation. Presumably, he desires to engage in an activity that brings him enjoyment simultaneously. It is highly likely that he is unable to afford the payment required for re-entry into the institution. The attainment of a realistic appearance is rendered intricate, in addition to the hesitancy to make premature commitments on expenditures.

That is the reason for his shortcomings.

Nevertheless, I do not presuppose that it is unquestionably a negative aspect. Many individuals do not easily conform to a predetermined trajectory. Achieving personal accomplishment through solitary efforts may lead to success; however, it is unlikely to result in true happiness.

This is the factor. In order to achieve both wealth and prestige in a conventional manner, it is advisable to select a specific path, preferably one that is widely accepted, and diligently pursue the manifestation of each step.

Alternatively, if your focus lies beyond material wealth or achievements, you may choose to carefully search for the ideal life.

Do not procrastinate excessively in making your decision. Each moment you contemplate is a minute you forfeit.

Visualization - Heaven's Fire

Visualization is the process of conjuring a mental representation through the creation of a visual image within one's mind. I firmly uphold that it stands as an integral cornerstone in harnessing the power of the Law of Attraction within our existence.

By incorporating visualization and channeling intense emotional energy into our concentrated intention, we effectively kindle the celestial flame within the image of our aspirations.

Our thoughts and reflections have the power to manifest in our reality. By engaging in the act of envisioning our desires, we effectively communicate to the Universe, prompting the materialization of our aspirations.

The subconscious mind readily perceives your imagery as authentic.

Our physical selves react to visual or auditory stimuli originating from our subconsciousness. As an illustration, suppose I were to prompt you to mentally envision the inviting aroma of newly baked bread or apple pie, exuding warmth and sweetness, resulting in a conditioned response akin to that observed in Pavlov's classical conditioning experiment, wherein salivation ensues. Your mind exhibits this reaction due to its inability to discern the distinction between reality and falsehood.

If one is acquainted with the flavor of an apple, their physiology registers the signals and recollection, prompting a response regardless of the authenticity of the pie, whether it is physically present or merely conceptualized. In a similar vein, should I request that you envision the tangy flavor of a ripe lemon, it is likely that you would instinctively pucker at the mere notion of its tartness.

Daydreams do not constitute deliberate focuses on specific visualizations. Daydreams encompass fanciful thoughts that gracefully drift akin to ethereal cumulus clouds within the realm of our consciousness. They lack clear purpose and are devoid of substance, rendering them incapable of attaching themselves to anything concrete. Our daydreams transpire fleetingly within the confines of our consciousness before dissipating. Daydreams can be regarded as brief fantasies that offer a temporary respite for the mind from the repetitive routines and engagements of daily life.

Infrequently, daydreams may yield outcomes, albeit solely when a sufficient amount of exertion is devoted to them.

Physical therapists have extensively conveyed that patients who engage in mental imagery of walking or moving exhibit expedited progress when compared to individuals who do not employ such techniques. Indeed, visualizations have been extensively documented as a effective means to enhance wellbeing, bolster physical stamina, and facilitate injury recovery.

There exist individuals who excel in sports, contemporary Olympians, and athletes across the globe who employ visualization techniques in order to enhance their physical prowess.

In order to manifest your aspiration on the material realm, it is imperative to possess a well-defined depiction of your desire within your mental faculties. Commence with the solution.

Suppose, momentarily, you desire to materialize a new automobile. To commence, articulately express your intention with fervor imbued in each word. Embrace the resonance of possessing the automobile of your aspirations and devote your emotional vitality towards visualizing this accomplishment.

Express gratitude as you envision operating your forthcoming vehicle and experiencing the sense of satisfaction that comes with possessing it. Ensure that you consistently conclude your visualization of affirmation. I currently witness the presence of this outcome or a more favorable one.

Upon reaching the point of acquiring a new automobile, I proceeded to reproduce an image of a Nissen Rogue and proceeded to encase it within a tasteful frame, which I subsequently positioned on my desk.

I dedicated time to envisioning my Rogue both in the morning and prior to retiring for the evening.

In addition, I incorporated conscious musings, mental imagery, and sentiments during my commute to and from work or while running errands. During that period, I channelled my emotional energy into the act of owning a car. Upon perceiving the sight of a Nissen Rogue, it would bring to mind the resemblance between that particular vehicle and my own car. Upon observing my vehicle reflected in the storefront window, I would envision an altered depiction featuring a Nissen Rogue. At intersections marked with red lights, I would express my gratitude through a simple affirmation, acknowledging my appreciation to the divine entity as the source of my newly acquired Nissen vehicle.

Harmonize your energy with the delight of possessing a brand-new automobile. Experience and deeply embrace the sheer delight that your new car brings when you take it for a drive. Conceive of your digits encircling the fresh steering wheel. Consider the effortless manoeuvrability and seamless deceleration that ensues, ensuring a secure halt. Consider the potential sensory experience of the new seats, appreciate the lustrous sheen of the elegant dashboard, and acknowledge the effortless maneuverability and parking capability. Envision the resonant sound emitted by your automobile upon engaging the automatic locking mechanism, as well as the aesthetic appeal it shall exude, enhancing the allure of your driveway or designated parking area.

Each instance that I contemplated my newly acquired automobile, I expressed my gratitude and permitted an immense sense of appreciation to surface within me, evoking an exhilarating sensation associated with possessing the Nissen. In final remarks, I would assert, "this or a more favorable outcome was destined to manifest in my life."

I never considered the manner in which my new car would manifest in my life. I have recently completed the visualization and manifestation process. In the following month, the very same automobile appeared in my driveway, accompanied by monthly installments that were comfortably within my financial means.

Through the duration of the day, establish connection with your visualization by means of demonstrating it through your behavior, speech, and deeds.

Kindly be aware that while engaging in any manifestation or visualization, it is imperative to adhere to the Universal principle of nonmaleficence. If your mental imagery encompasses intentions to engage in theft, deception, or extramarital conduct, you will inevitably become entangled in unfavorable karmic repercussions. Do no harm.

Embrace a mindset in which you conduct your life in alignment with the reality you desire, and you shall witness its tangible manifestation unfold at an accelerated pace beyond the bounds of your imagination.

Conclude your Visualization by stating, "This manifestation or a superior outcome is now materializing in my life," and declare, "Amen" or "And thus it shall be!"

As one progresses through the various chapters of this book, a multitude of visualizations shall be discovered, allowing for utilization, adaptation, or the ability to generate one's own.

Strive to render your visualization with the highest degree of realism. Incorporating the five senses into your imagery forms part of this endeavor. The five senses encompass the faculties of vision, auditory perception, olfaction, gustation, and tactile sensation.

As an author specializing in the genres of mystery and romantic suspense, my aim is to incorporate a comprehensive range of sensory details into every scene. In the event that my protagonist descends the staircase, I shall depict her action of gently caressing the banister, utilizing a phrase such as "she delicately trailed her fingertips along the crest of the railing, briefly enthralled by the polished and refreshing sensation of the wooden surface."

I kindly request that you replicate this approach in your visualization. Within every visual representation during the course of your meditation, engage all of your five senses. For example, suppose you are envisioning yourself at the seaside. Take a moment to envisage the invigorating aroma of the saline breeze, attend to the piercing cries of seagulls soaring above the undulating waves, perceive the sensation of coarse particles underfoot, or recognize the gentle caress of a strand of hair swaying across your cheek.

You enhance the vividness of your imagery by incorporating the sensory perceptions of sight, sound, aroma, flavor, and tactility. The greater degree to which you authenticate this visual representation, the stronger your connection with it becomes, accelerating your mental acceptance of the image, and consequently expediting the Universe's responsiveness to it.

The subsequent passage outlines my comprehensive manual for visualization. The more fervently you invest emotional energy into the intricacies, the more expeditious the realization of your aspirations will be.

Preventative Measures For Averting Common Drawbacks In Visualizations

Enemies Of Visualization

The incorporation of visualization is a pivotal component as it has the potential to yield significant impact on an individual's level of achievement. The optimal performance is minimally influenced by distractions and extraneous incentives. You must be conscious of the fact that certain factors can impede visualization and pose challenges along your path to success.

Focus on the technical aspects of the abilities. Give attention to the operational aspects of the skills. Direct your efforts to the practical elements of the abilities.

Proficiency demands a profound level of competence, after which one must transition into a state of preconsciousness. The efficacy of movement execution may be diminished by the act of visualizing each motion, as it modulates one's cognitive focus away from pertinent tasks and objectives.

Residence of Inner Emotions and Weary Atmosphere.

It is crucial to monitor the internal state through introspection, but becoming preoccupied with these inner emotions hinders one's ability to focus on external visualization. For success in their workout, it is necessary for both a man and a woman to possess a shared attribute that helps them ward off fatigue and pain. To effectively utilize your cognitive abilities, it is crucial to engage in visualization techniques in order to address and alleviate exhaustion. By keeping a psychological distance from distressing thoughts, such as those related to injury and other sources of pain, you will bolster your ability to overcome limitations and accomplish significant feats.

Entertaining Nonproductive Self-Talk

Internal dialogue is an innate characteristic of human consciousness, but the content and characteristics of this dialogue can vary. Adverse self-dialogue has the potential to detrimentally impact your performance and disrupt your focus. Individuals are advised to give due focus to positive thoughts, as it has been observed that fearful thoughts can have an adverse impact on one's self-assurance. In order to uphold your visualization, carry out optimal actions, and sustain motivation, it is imperative to engage in the practice of visualizing positive and productive conversations effectively. Over time, this method will prove to be highly effective in regulating your thoughts.

Retrospective Visualization

In order to sustain a state of well-being in your perception, it is crucial to actively immerse yourself in optimistic thinking and behaviors. The detrimental impact of your negative actions and behaviors on your ability to visualize is considerable, as your thoughts consistently remain occupied with past failures and irrelevant pursuits. It is anticipated that this will lead to a decrease in motivation levels, ultimately impairing overall performance. It is necessary to focus on visualizing your present circumstances rather than immersing your thoughts in the actual experience. It is advisable to employ the technique of visualization in both the planning and risk management stages.

Envisioning the Future

Contemplating the potential outcomes and rewards of a given task, and envisaging one's future progress, may impede one's performance. In order to cultivate a prosperous future, it is imperative to engage in visualizing the present moment while relinquishing unnecessary contemplation of future possibilities. Maintain focused attention and exert maximum effort in accordance with the requirements, avoiding preoccupation with the potential results.

Obstacles Presented by Visual and Auditory Diversions

Engaging in social and electronic activities can divert your attention, as you may become prone to distraction by various stimuli. Sustaining focus and concentration may prove challenging due to the presence of numerous external stimuli that can interrupt cognitive processes. You must cultivate your concentration skills through concerted efforts to eliminate the various distractions that permeate your daily existence. Eliminate distractions as they have the potential to impede your visualization process. The electronic devices have the potential to entice individuals into using them. In order to utilize the technique of visualization effectively, it is imperative to minimize distractions caused by electronic devices by disabling them and thereby preventing interruptions from the audible notifications they produce. Ensure that you prioritize your mental acuity, as it is indispensable for the sustenance of focus and self-awareness.

Distractions

Distraction refers to the state of having one's attention divided, thereby disrupting the focus on routine activities. One's consciousness may be disturbed by an occurrence, an item, a collective of individuals, and visual stimuli. If one possesses an inadequate capacity for attentiveness, it would correspondingly pose challenges to sustain visualization proficiency. There exist numerous external and internal factors that have the potential to undermine one's attentiveness. Distractibility refers to a cognitive condition wherein individuals encounter challenges in sustaining their mental imagery.

3-Advanced Visualizations Tools

Allow us to explore a selection of cutting-edge data visualization tools:

Openheatmap

Using this tool, it is possible to effortlessly convert your spreadsheet, particularly one containing geographical data, into a fully operational heat map with a mere click of a button. Openheatmap requires that you have your data stored in a Google Spreadsheet, therefore you will need to transfer your data from an Excel spreadsheet to a Google Spreadsheet. This process can be deemed insignificant in comparison to the outcomes that the tool will yield.

Leaflet

This tool may not be suitable for those who are new to the field, as it is a JavaScript library that should be integrated into one's data visualization framework. Nevertheless, a favorable aspect of this tool resides in its lightweight nature, boasting a mere 33 KB in size. The tool not only generates maps, but also produces interactive maps that are well-suited for mobile devices. The fact that Leaflet possesses this capability outshines even certain commercial data visualization tools, highlighting the immense strength of the former. If you possess a preference for employing the command line tool or engaging in the creation of an Application Programming Interface (API), it is advisable to opt for the Leaflet library.

Chartbuilder

This chart creation tool, which gained popularity, was developed and made accessible by Quartz, a financial news website, in the year 2013. Quartz had devised the tool for internal utilization by its journalists for the purpose of augmenting the visual presentation of their news stories. Nevertheless, the Chartbuilder tool lacks visual appeal in its standalone form and presents challenges for novice users. It is mandatory for you to possess the knowledge to effectively download, install, and activate a Python script within the designated tool.

Nonetheless, once the installation process is complete, all that will be required is the replication and insertion of your data into the designated tool. Consequently, you will gain the ability to generate graphical representations that can be further customized according to your preferred style sheets. Nevertheless, the tool possesses a drawback in that it fails to produce interactive graphics to the same extent as other tools do. The tool is exclusively designed for generating highly polished static charts with utmost ease, requiring only a few steps.

Open Refine

Many individuals tend to disregard the significance of data transformation, a process that proves highly beneficial in the context of data visualization. This feature proves to be particularly advantageous when obtaining data from various sources, including spreadsheets and logs that record extensive transactions derived from machine learning algorithms, among others.

Data transformation involves the systematic conversion of a heterogeneous collection of numerical values into cohesive and interconnected data points. Consequently, data is subject to a thorough cleansing process, subsequently undergoing transformation and ultimately becoming accessible to external tools, such as web pages. If you consistently encounter challenges with these tasks, it would be advisable for you to utilize the Open Refine tool. It originated as a subsidiary of Google, but it has since transitioned into an independent entity. If you possess a multitude of disparate data at your disposal, we recommend employing this tool to enhance the data.

Google Data Studio

The Google Data Studio is a part of Google Marketing platforms that enables users to generate diverse perspectives of their data and dashboards, rather than solely producing visualizations for one-time use and publication. Nevertheless, its usage presents a certain level of complexity, necessitating an individual to undergo a learning curve in order to achieve proficiency. Seamless integration with the Google Analytics tool is achievable.

Plotly

This particular tool exhibits a higher level of intricacy in comparison to Tableau, accompanied by noteworthy analytical advantages. This application enables users to generate charts using R and Python, along with the capability to develop personalized data analytics applications utilizing Python. In addition, it possesses the capability of seamless integration with extensive and freely available libraries for R, Python, and JavaScript.

Kibana

This particular feature is a vital element within the Elastic Stack framework as it facilitates the process of transforming data into meaningful visual representations, thereby enabling the extraction of valuable insights. It was specifically designed and developed solely for utilization with Elasticsearch data. Nevertheless, Kibana remains the optimal solution for the visual representation of log data.

This tool facilitates the creation of various data visualization techniques, encompassing interactive maps, charts, histograms, and numerous other forms. This tool also surpasses conventional dashboards for data analytics and visualization.

By leveraging Kibana, users have the ability to construct sophisticated analytics, integrate visualizations derived from diverse sources, in order to investigate novel associations between disparate insights, and ultimately employ machine learning capabilities to discover concealed patterns and relationships encompassing data events.

Subconscious Mind And Visualization

The subconscious mind governs our behavioral responses and influences our individual characteristics. It determines our transformation. Another intriguing aspect of the subconscious mind lies in its ability to draw in favorable circumstances. There are numerous indications that the subconscious mind possesses the ability to draw towards us the conditions and qualities we desire in our lives. Once we have made a conscious decision to acquire something and effectively convey our intentions to the subconscious, it will draw towards us circumstances that are advantageous to our desires, thereby manifesting them into reality. What is the method of establishing communication with the subconscious mind? Regrettably, the mode of reception pertaining to the subconscious differs from that of the conscious mind. The conscious mind operates and engages in communication through the use of verbal language. The subconscious mind, nonetheless, conveys messages via visual means. Yes, it functions effectively when applied to images. This is the role that visualization plays. We direct our subconscious mind through the use of visualization. Consistent implementation of mental imagery will naturally draw towards us all the circumstances and qualities that we desire in our lives. The subconscious functions akin to a magnet. Furthermore, we can enhance the effectiveness of visualization by employing a specific type of auditory stimulus to stimulate our subconscious mind. The sound has been validated by scientific evidence and is readily accessible to consumers in the market. Applying this particular auditory stimulus amplifies the influence on the subconscious mind, fostering heightened stimulation during the process of visualization. We mentally construct our desired outcomes in all domains for approximately thirty minutes while concurrently playing the accompanying audio. The more distinct the image we perceive, the greater allure we will garner. The optimal period for engaging in visualization is during the morning prior to commencing work and in the evening preceding bedtime. Consistently engaging in visualization exercises on a daily basis will not merely provide you with determination, but will also impart energy and vitality.

The potential of our brain can be remarkably potent in determining our success in life, provided that we possess a comprehensive understanding and adeptness in harnessing its capabilities. The stimulation of the subconscious mind yields results that surpass imagination. Having the ability to employ it alongside suitable visualization is a surefire recipe for achieving success in our lives.

Visualization Decoded

In order for visualization to effectively materialize one's desires, it is imperative to possess a well-defined concept from the outset. Let us consider a scenario where you are required to mentally conceptualize or imagine the appearance of a chair. Initially, you would conceptualize the desired aesthetic of the chair in your mind. In the event of uncertainty, one could peruse alternative chairs, potentially amalgamating various components in order to construct a mental representation of the desired chair. Once you have achieved a comprehensive mental representation, you have successfully accomplished the fundamental stage of visualization.

Many individuals encounter difficulty at this juncture due to the subsequent proliferation of possibilities. There are numerous methods through which the chair can be embodied. The item in question may take various forms, such as a chair received as a gift, bought, or presented to another individual. Receiving gifts is a delightful experience; however, it represents just one avenue through which the universe manifests your desires. By fixating on obtaining what you desire from others, you inadvertently surrender your own autonomy and authority. One starts seeking external sources to fulfill their needs, thereby potentially experiencing a sense of powerlessness and despair.

This is additionally a contributing factor that renders it challenging to have faith in the attainment of your desires, as the outcome hinges not upon your own capabilities, but rather on the actions and circumstances controlled by external agents. The preponderance of things that are materialized can be classified under the aforementioned two categories, namely, they are either acquired through an exchange involving monetary or temporal resources, or they are brought into existence through creative endeavors.

In order to acquire the chair, it is advisable to mentally visualize the image of said chair whilst searching for retail establishments that offer comparable chair models. You are welcome to conduct a search either on the internet or visit a physical retail establishment until you locate the item, at which point you may engage in a transaction involving an exchange of goods or currency in order to acquire it. Typically, the ultimate category in which the foremost desires of individuals lie is that of their creation. This encompasses an array of elements, ranging from harmonious personal relationships, thriving enterprises, a meaningful existence, enhanced well-being, and more.

This is indeed a positive development, as the emergence of these entities provides individuals with the ability to exert their own creative agency. After achieving a clear visualization of your desired outcome, what steps must be taken to bring it into fruition? This is the point where you employ the most potent method of visualization, leveraging your innate ability to visualize in order to manifest your aspirations into tangible existence. Proceed with the act of mental imagery, employing the technique of creative visualization.

When one possesses a well-defined mental representation or portrayal of the chair desired, one has effectively instantiated an imaginative construct through the employment of creative visualization. You sought guidance from your mental faculties on the means to manifest that visual in your present circumstances. As an illustration, in order to construct the chair, it would be advisable to retain a mental representation of the chair while actively seeking the requisite materials and tools for its fabrication. Consider the necessary tools and materials to effectively observe and contemplate the thoughts that arise. Ponder upon your requirements and deliberate on the manner in which you intend to utilize said resources. Allow your mind to do the heavy lifting. In the contemporary era characterized by rapid advancements, the opportunity to engage in thoughtful contemplation and strategic deliberation can often be perceived as a privilege. It is more convenient to opt for the initial option that presents itself and endure the resulting difficulties. Speed through the task and witness its eventual collapse, subsequently questioning the reasons behind its failure. You assign responsibility to oneself or engage in self-defeating narratives, where you convince yourself of the impossibility of achieving your desires. When one refrains from affording themselves an opportunity to manifest their genuine desires.

Envision the process by which you could accomplish this task, considering the sequential actions required to reach the end goal. Envision yourself engaging in the process of constructing that chair. In order to achieve that manifestation, it would be necessary to possess the necessary tools and proficiency. In consideration of each phase of the project, the initial course of action would involve deliberate contemplation of the tasks at hand. Please contemplate the optimal approach for accomplishing this task. Refrain from embracing ideas that lack constructive value. Consider conceptualizing each successive action, thereby affording yourself the opportunity to experiment with different approaches that yield successful outcomes. Once the most exceptional idea has been conceived, one's perspective on how to successfully execute it will become notably more lucid. Kindly ensure that you do not overlook the need to take prompt action. The efficacy of creative visualization is contingent upon its concurrent integration with action. Particularly when venturing into uncharted territory to forge new accomplishments, it is imperative to embrace the principles of adaptability, embracing transformation, and fostering personal development. An integral aspect of the learning process involves uncovering both successful and unsuccessful strategies, should one encounter an approach that proves unsuccessful. Conduct a thorough analysis of the matter at hand, contemplating the reasons behind its failure and considering alternative approaches that would yield successful outcomes. Observe the functioning of your mind, permit yourself to contemplate it, and perceive the operations of your mind. You may observe that you engage in the contemplation of various scenarios within your thoughts. This exemplifies the pinnacle of creative visualization through persistent dedication, enabling you to establish the most pragmatic approach to materializing the life you yearn for.

One has the ability to influence their own fate, and the fundamental factor in shaping one's life resides internally rather than externally. Mastering your thoughts is vital to harnessing the power of the Law of Attraction.

The Transformative Impact Of Creative Visualization: A Comparative Examination Of Case Studies

As previously stated, through the application of creative visualization, individuals have the ability to personally mold and construct their lives in alignment with their aspirations and ambitions.

Creative visualization can be classified as a form of cognitive encoding. In essence, as you consistently or repeatedly project any mental image within a compartment of your mind, the subconscious mind duly recognizes this mental image, inducing you to think and act in alignment with these images instinctively.

This provides a compelling rationale for the recommendation to solely focus on envisioning favorable outcomes and endeavors that have the potential to enhance one's life.

Additionally, remarkable outcomes arise from the act of visualizing. Curious to learn how? After the continual or regular prediction of the mental image in your subconscious, one eventually begins to perceive an external reality that was previously unexperienced - that is, through this preexisting image that has been formed.

This implies that you will commence behaving in accordance with the mental representation. In essence, it can be likened to a cognitive rehearsal that shapes one's perspective, behaviors, and tendencies. No matter the nature of the thoughts that may consume your mind, be they positive or negative, you will inevitably gravitate towards them.

Inevitably, through the implementation of creative visualization, a multitude of opportunities are thriving. Throughout one's lifetime, there exist numerous actions that can be undertaken to diligently enhance one's overall state of well-being. There exists a multitude of individuals who possess the capacity to nurture or inspire you towards your inevitable destination.

Visualization has the capacity to expand one's cognitive faculties, enabling them to perceive, recognize, and capitalize on these opportunities. For instance, you desire a specific occupation, yet your rational faculties are persuading you that it is unattainable.

It conveys the message that you do not possess the necessary qualifications for obtaining a job of that nature, leaving you with a sense of unworthiness for such a position. This idea will dissuade you from actively seeking and anticipating acquisition of the aforementioned employment opportunity.

Alternatively, if one were to envision themselves performing the duties of said occupation and their subconscious mind were to acknowledge this visualization, gradually they would develop a belief in their ability to attain said job and proceed to undertake the requisite steps in acquiring said position.

We have encountered numerous celebrities who assert that the utilization of creative visualization has served as a driving force behind their achievements. Distinguished individuals such as Oprah, Tiger Woods, Will Smith, Arnold Schwarzenegger, Bill Gates, and numerous others have prominently expressed their utilization of the technique of visualization to overcome adversities and manifest their long-held aspirations well in advance of their actual fulfillment.

There have been speculations suggesting that Jim Carrey allegedly issued a personal check to himself for the amount of 10 million dollars, long before his financial status warranted such a transaction. Nevertheless, his subconsciousness recognized and accepted the fact that he would acquire that sum of money. He persisted in engaging in mental imagery for an extended period of time, until the year 1974 when he was awarded a staggering sum of 10 million dollars in acknowledgment of his performance in the acclaimed film, Dump And Dumper. This serves as the most evident manifestation of the efficacy of creative visualization.

Arnold Schwarzenegger expressed that prior to his initial triumph in the Mr. Universe competition, he carried himself with an air of regality akin to Mufasa surveying his domain. In his perspective, he had emerged victorious on numerous occasions. As a result of this, his subconscious mind became accustomed to success, ultimately leading to his achievement.

He once more ventured into the film industry, employing the identical strategy of visualizing himself as a highly successful actor and reaping substantial financial rewards, ultimately achieving his goals. Arnold's ideology posits that one's mindset plays a crucial role in their eventual success.

Camille Duvall, an accomplished water skier, asserts that she employed the technique of creative visualization to engage her mental faculties during the dawn of competitions. Prior to getting out of bed, she mentally visualized herself executing impressive runs with exceptional mastery of techniques.

Throughout her thought process, based on her highest personal effort, she asserts that the greater your ability to mentally picture things in this manner, ultimately, you will commence experiencing the harmonious activation of your muscles at the appropriate moments.

Now, let us turn our attention to exploring strategic approaches for engaging in the practice of creative visualization.